SOMEONE WITH YOU

"I am with you. That is all you need."

2 CORINTHIANS 12:9

Someone

with You

BY LARRY LIBBY

ILLUSTRATED BY SERGIO MARTINEZ

GOLD'N'HONEY BOOKS

WHEN YOU'RE ASKED TO DO SOMETHING VERY, VERY HARD

Remember, God is with you

When Peter first stuck his foot over the edge of the boat and stepped onto the water, he knew he couldn't do it.

Of course he couldn't! Who ever heard of someone walking on water? Walking on ice, maybe, or walking *under* water. But taking a hike across the sea? Well...how could that be?

But here he was...just about to step out over the side of the boat into the night and the storm and the waves. My goodness, how had an old fisherman gotten himself into such a fix? Here's what the Bible says:

> Then Jesus made his followers get into the boat. He told them to go ahead of him to the other side of the lake. Jesus...went alone up into the hills to pray. It was late, and Jesus was there alone. By this time, the boat was already far away on the lake. The boat was having trouble because of the waves, and the wind was blowing against it.
>
> Between three and six o'clock in the morning, Jesus' followers were still in the boat. Jesus came to them. He was walking on the water. When the followers saw him walking on the water, they were afraid. They said, "It's a ghost!" and cried out in fear.
>
> But Jesus quickly spoke to them. He said, "Have courage! It is I! Don't be afraid."
>
> Peter said, "Lord, if that is really you, then tell me to come to you on the water."
> (Matthew 14:22–28)

Now, I imagine there had been plenty of times when Peter *wished* he could walk on water. Maybe he'd been out on the Sea of Galilee and remembered leaving a very nice sack lunch on the beach. After all the trouble Mrs. Peter had gone to fix it, too! It would have been too far to row back, and if there's no wind, the sail's no good, either.

Oh, but if he could vault over the side of the boat and *jog* right over the water to the shore, he could grab his cheese sandwiches and be back in time to check his fish nets. And wouldn't that cool water feel great on the bottom of hot bare feet?

Or what if Peter got stuck out in the sea with some annoying old fisherman named Zadab who was trying to talk his ear off? I'll bet Peter liked a little peace and quiet while he was fishing. (I know I do!) Most fishermen enjoy time out in their boats to think about things. But what do you do if you're stuck with someone like ol' Zadab? What do you do if you're out to sea with someone who keeps bragging about how many fish he's caught and what great boats he's owned and how wise and clever he is (and on and on)?

I can imagine Peter wishing he could step over the side of the boat, say, "So sorry, Zadab. I've got to run," and tramp quickly back over the water to shore.

But those sorts of thoughts would only be wishes, wouldn't they? Imaginary things. Nobody could *really* walk on water.

But there was Jesus
...out in the stormy night
...standing on the churning sea.
There was Jesus
...the wild wind blowing through His hair
...His robe flapping behind Him
...His hand outstretched.
And what was He shouting over the crash of waves and howl of wind?

"COME."

Come?

Jesus wanted Peter to get out of the boat and *step onto the water?* Without a life jacket? Without a scuba tank? Without fins and a snorkel? That wasn't going to be very easy, was it?

Peter left the boat and walked on the water to Jesus. But when Peter saw the wind and the waves, he became afraid and began to sink. He shouted, "Lord, save me!"

Then Jesus reached out his hand and caught Peter. Jesus said, "Your faith is small. Why did you doubt?" (Matthew 14:29–31)

Now, Peter knew he couldn't walk on water. But just for a moment, when his eyes were fixed on Jesus, it didn't matter what he thought he could do or couldn't do. What mattered was what the Lord had *told* him to do. And Peter knew in an instant that if Jesus said "Do it," he could do it.

But then, out there on that water doing what he would never do on his own, he suddenly told himself, "I can't do this!" And just that quickly, the water that had felt so firm the moment before suddenly felt like regular old water and he started to plunge right through it.

His prayer, *"Lord, save me!"* is one of the shortest and best prayers in all the Bible. (If you're ever in trouble and that's the only prayer you can remember or have time for, it works very well.)

Has the Lord ever asked you to do something you thought you couldn't do? Something that frightened you? Something that seemed too big and too hard for you?

What if you told a lie and Jesus said, "I want you to go to the person you lied to and tell him the real truth"? Oh boy, that's hard!

What if you took something that wasn't yours and Jesus said, "I want you to take back that thing and admit what you've done"? That's even harder!

What if He said to you, "I want you to talk to that boy or that girl in your class about Me"? You might want to say, "Oh, I could NEVER talk to HIM about Jesus" or "I could NEVER tell HER that I love the Lord! That would be way too hard for me!"

But if Jesus asks you to do it, then you really *can* do it...or else

He would never have asked you, right? You can do anything He asks you to do, if He is there with you.

This is how that Bible story ends:

After Peter and Jesus were in the boat, the wind became calm. Then those who were in the boat worshiped Jesus and said, "Truly you are the Son of God!" (Matthew 14:32–33)

That's the point, isn't it? If He is the Son of God (and He is!), then *nothing* is too hard for Him. And if He is with you, helping you to do what you could never do before, nothing is too hard for you, either.

If *He* says you can do it, you can do it!
And that's all there is to it.

WHEN YOU FEEL LIKE GOD IS FAR AWAY

Remember, God is with you

All of this talk about God being "with me" is fine, but...good grief, isn't He really far, far away? He created the whole universe, right to its very edges. (Wouldn't it be fun to take a peek at the very edge of the universe? I wonder what it looks like. Would its edge be ragged or smooth—or just sort of fade away? I wonder what's just six inches on the other side of it.) There's so much I don't know. But I do know that if God created everything there is, it means He is beyond and above it all.

That's pretty far away from me...isn't it?

All of this talk about God being "with me" is nice, but...my goodness, isn't He so very much greater than I am?

If our sun can hold a million earths, and some of the most massive stars can hold thousands of our sun, and the great galaxies of deep space can hold trillions of those stars, and if there are more of these galaxies than anyone could begin to count...well, what am I? I'm just a grain of sand on an endless beach. I'm just one little leaf blowing along on a night wind. I'm so very tiny, and to be as powerful as He is, God must be very, VERY LARGE.

That means He's far away from me...doesn't it?

All of this talk about God being "with me" has its place, I guess, but...oh man! He's so good and pure and holy, and I'm not! He is perfect and sinless and spotless, and the beauty of His character blazes white hot—like the furnace heart of a great star. And me? Well, I'm always falling short. I'm always missing the mark. I'm always stubbing my toe. I'm always getting muddied and muddled and stained.

That means He's far away from me...doesn't it?

All of this talk about God being "with me" sounds nice and all that, but...wow! He's sitting on some throne in *Heaven*. And where is Heaven?

Who knows? It's someplace beyond anyplace that we know. It's beautiful beyond imagining and vast beyond words. And it's filled up with great crowds of shining angels and all those who have trusted God and Jesus down through the ages. And me? Well, I live in a plain old house in a plain old neighborhood in a plain old town here on earth.

That has to mean He is far, far away from me...right?

What then, did Jesus mean when He said to His followers:

> "If you love me, you will do the things I command. I will ask the Father, and he will give you another Helper. He will give you this Helper to be with you forever. The Helper is the Spirit of truth. The world cannot accept him because it does not see him or know him. But you know him. He lives with you and he will be in you." (John 14:15–17)

The Holy Spirit is God, just as Jesus and the Father are God. And the Bible says He is with me forever? He is with me and *in* me? Does that mean that GOD—the Almighty Creator and King of kings—somehow lives inside ME? And that He is my Helper?

Then...

He really isn't far away, is He? He really couldn't be much *closer*, could He?

He's as close as my skin.

He's as close as my thoughts.

He's as close as my next breath.

He's as close as my secret dreams.

He's as close as my deepest longings.

He's as close as the beat of my heart.

And He is with me here RIGHT NOW.

If you think I understand all of this—or even very much of it—you're wrong. But if you think that *believing* this makes me thankful and just happy to be alive, you're right as you can be!

God is

never far away!

WHEN EVERYTHING SEEMS TO GO WRONG

Remember, God is with you

An African-American friend of mine named Ken told me about the time he played Little League baseball, down in Alabama.

Ken grew up in a poor neighborhood, and none of the boys had enough money for uniforms. To raise some funds, the team decided to sell boxes of candy door to door. One boy named Maynard was the best little salesman of all, and he sold more candy than anyone else. As a matter of fact, he was so successful and busy at selling candy, he didn't have much time to practice baseball.

On the day of their first game, the team was terribly proud of their new uniforms. Oh, these guys looked *good!* They might not have practiced very much, but they looked really sharp in those new red hats, crisp, red-numbered jerseys, and flashy baseball pants with big red stripes running down the legs.

Maynard was SO excited. All his hard work had paid off. He looked like a real baseball player! The other team was up to bat first, and Maynard was out in center field—I mean *way* out there. He was a little nervous, because he wasn't sure what to do. (That's the way it is when you don't practice.) But he probably felt safe because NO ONE would be able to hit the ball out as far as he was anyway.

But right off the bat, someone *did* hit it that far.

The very first batter on the very first pitch smacked a high pop fly that seemed to climb all day into the hazy summer sky. Finally it began arching down again.

Right toward center field.

Right toward Maynard.

Maynard yelled, "I got it! I got it!" and stuck his glove in the air over his head.

Now, that was the right thing to do, but maybe the wrong time to do it. With his big mitt in front of his face, Maynard could no longer see where the ball was. And the longer he waited for it to come down, the more nervous he became. *Where was that thing? What was taking it so long?*

Maynard had to find out. He dropped his glove (just for a moment) to get his eye back on the ball. The ball, however, arrived just as Maynard lowered his glove. *Crack!* The ball smacked him hard, right on top of the head.

Maynard screamed and grabbed his head, knocking his new red hat into the Alabama dust. Then he threw down his glove and ran right out of the ball field, heading for home and mama, crying all the way.

"Maynard, wait!" his teammates called. "Where are you going?"

"I quit!" Maynard yelled. "I QUIT!"

So he quit the team after the very first pitch of the very first game...even after all his hard work and all of his excitement and all those boxes of candy.

That was too soon to quit!

If he had just waited for a while on the bench, his head might have felt better. With a lot of practice he could have become better. He might even have *caught* the next ball and begun to enjoy the game. He might have learned alongside his teammates and had the fun of growing together with his team. Instead of just looking like a baseball player, Maynard could have *become* a baseball player. And who knows? Maybe even a good one.

Sometimes people give up way too soon. I know of kids who gave up way too soon on a commitment they had made. I know of moms and dads who gave up way too soon on a marriage. I know of Christians who gave up praying for someone, thinking he or she would never change, or accept the Lord Jesus as Savior. And maybe saddest of all, I know of a teenage boy who gave up on his own *life* because he'd put a dent in his dad's pickup truck.

Yes, there are times when things look so very bad, so very dark and hopeless. But when you have Jesus in your life, things can never *really* be hopeless. Do you know why that is? The apostle Paul calls

the Lord "Christ Jesus our hope" (1 Timothy 1:1). And that's just what He is.

HE IS OUR HOPE.

Many of the things that you and I hope for never come to be. We feel disappointed and let down. Our hopes are like the flames of little candles on a birthday cake. One good blow, and out they go in a puff of smoke. But when we put our hope in Jesus, the fire can *never* be put out. There isn't a storm or a hurricane or a tornado in all the world that can blow out *that* flame!

When He says He will be with us, HE WILL BE WITH US.

When He says He will never leave us, HE WILL NEVER LEAVE US.

When He says He will take us to Heaven when we die, HE WILL DO IT!

And nothing can ever make Him change His mind about something He has promised.

Don't ever give up! Because Jesus your Hope will *never* give up on you.

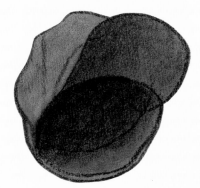

WHEN YOU HAVE HURTS THAT WON'T GO AWAY

Remember, God is with you

The best thing about getting hurt is how good it feels when it stops hurting. And most hurts stop after a while, don't they? If you bang your knee, it hurts like crazy—at first. But most of the time, you can count to a hundred and the hurt will fade away. When you step on a bee with bare feet (and I don't mean the *bee* has bare feet), the sting can go on for several hours before it stops.

But what if you had a hurt that didn't stop at all?

What if it were there all day every day, and all night every night? Can you imagine such a thing? Some people have to live with hurts like that.

And not all hurts are outside hurts, either. Some of the worst hurts are *inside* hurts: hurt feelings, hurts of the heart. And these may be hurts that stay and stay, even though we want them to go away.

In the Bible, the apostle Paul talked to God about his hurt.

It bothered him so much he called it a "thorn in my flesh." (Ouch!) In a letter to some friends, Paul wrote: "I begged God three times to make me well again. Each time he said, 'No. But I am with you. That is all that you need. My power shows up best in weak people'" (2 Corinthians 12:8—9, SLB).

Then do you know what Paul said?

> Now I am glad to brag about how weak I am. I am glad
> to show off Christ's power instead of my own. Now I
> know it is all for Christ's good.
> (2 Corinthians 12:9—10, SLB)

Use your imagination with me for a moment, okay?

Let's imagine that you had a hurt foot—hurt so badly that you couldn't even walk. That would be a hard thing to live with, wouldn't it? But as long as we're imagining things, let's imagine you had your very own angel (maybe his name could be Skye) whose only job every day was to carry you around through the air on his wide, strong shoulders.

Wow! Wouldn't that be neat? Skye would meet you in the morning, just as you were rubbing the sleep out of your eyes. "Get out from under those covers, Sleepyhead," he would say. "Where shall we go today?" (I don't really know if angels talk like that at all.)

And then the two of you would take off on all sorts of grand adventures and fly around to places no one has ever been before. (Angels must know tons of places like that.)

Would you still be sorry for your hurt foot? Would you still be sorry that you couldn't walk? Well, yes, I'm sure you would be. But it wouldn't be so very bad, really, if you had your own private angel to be with you and help you and take you on adventures.

But I know something even better than that.

The Lord Jesus Christ has promised to be with you ALWAYS—right up until the end of the world, and then for always after that. And He is a better, more powerful, more wonderful Friend than a million angels (any angel would quickly tell you that himself).

The Lord Jesus LOVES you, and the Bible doesn't say for sure if angels are even able to love people.

What's more, He is *with* you. He is with you in all the hurts of life.

The old hurts and the new hurts.
The big hurts and the little hurts.
The hurts that fade and the hurts that stay.
The inside hurts and the outside hurts.
The hurts others know about and the hurts
only you and God know about.

He meets you every morning—and that's an easy thing for Him to do, because He's already been with you all night!

Someday in Heaven, if you ever meet an angel named Skye, he will want to hear all about the way Jesus was with you in your hurts.

He'll probably make you tell it a million times. Angels never get tired of hearing about God's love for you and me, even though they can't understand it.

To tell the truth, I'm not sure I understand it, either.

But that's the good part. I don't *have* to understand it, I just have to believe it.

WHEN PEOPLE TREAT YOU MEAN AND TELL LIES ABOUT YOU

Remember, God is with you

When Mr. Lofton said he wanted to talk to me out in the hall, I felt a cold little wave of fear. Why would he want me to come out into the hall?

Why did he close the door behind us?

Why did he have that stiff, stern look on his face?

I really liked Mr. Lofton. He was the sixth grade teacher everyone wanted—maybe the best teacher at River Road School, except for Mrs. Walkenshaw, who was the best anywhere ever. He was really good in science and had neat stuff in the classroom, like model dinosaurs, a dead snake in a jar of formaldehyde, a cow eyeball in another jar, tarantulas and lizards, and that kind of thing.

I had never been in trouble in his class before, but I knew he could be tough when he had to be. (In my school, teachers used to *paddle* rowdy kids, and I saw Mr. Lofton break a paddle over Bob Jastead's backside. I think Bob had something hard in his back pocket.)

But this wasn't Bob Jastead goofing around again; Mr. Lofton wanted to see *me*. Out in the hall. And he looked angry.

I looked in his hand and saw that he was holding a couple of library books. But why would he want to show me those? Were they overdue or something?

Then he opened one of them. When he showed me one of the pages, I couldn't believe my eyes. Someone had taken a pen and drawn a picture on one of the pages. It wasn't a nice picture at all. To tell you the truth, it was a very dirty picture.

Worse than that, at the bottom of the picture it said *By Larry Libby*! And there were several pictures like that in each of the books. All of them said *By Larry Libby* at the bottom.

It even looked a lot like the way I signed my name in cursive, with big loops on the *L*s.

But I hadn't done it!

"I know that you like to draw cartoons, Larry," Mr. Lofton said. (It was true. I even had a drawing club with Steve Maricle and John Samms. We called it MSL Productions.) "So I just need you to explain this to me. *Did you do this?*"

It was awful! That wasn't the kind of cartoon I liked to draw at all. Why would anyone try to get me in trouble like that? Why would anyone sign my name under such ugly pictures?

It was a LIE!

Have you ever had someone tell a lie about you? Or have you ever had someone who didn't believe you were telling the truth—when you really were?

In times like those, it's good to remember that God knows our hearts. And even if everybody in the whole world turns against us and tells lies about us, God knows the truth, and He will always stand beside us. And having *God* stand beside you is better than having the whole world stand beside you.

Do you remember what the Lord Jesus told His followers about Himself? He said, "I am the way. And I am the TRUTH and the life" (John 14:6). You see, truth is not only something true, Truth is also a person. And that person is Jesus.

He is TRUTH.

He is THE Truth.

He is ALL Truth.

Everything about Him is true and right. Whatever truth there is in the world is His truth. He has never told a lie and never believed a lie. Lies can't even get close to Him—it would be like trying to drag some darkness up alongside the sun.

Once some evil, jealous men told lies about a young Christian named Stephen. They were such awful lies that a crowd of people became very angry and wanted to kill Stephen. But even when they were knocking Stephen down and throwing rocks at him, he forgave them.

Before he died, Stephen looked up at the sky. And guess who he saw?

He saw...THE TRUTH.

The Bible says:

> But Stephen was full of the Holy Spirit. He looked
> up to heaven and saw the glory of God. He saw Jesus
> standing at God's right side. He said, "Look! I see
> heaven open. And I see the Son of Man standing at
> God's right side!" (Acts 7:55−56)

In that moment, Stephen knew that Jesus was with him and that he was soon going to be in Heaven with Him. Jesus was even standing up to welcome him home! After that, all of the lies in the world couldn't hurt Stephen. When the TRUTH is with you— the shining, radiant, wonderful, true Son of God—the lies will soon fade away. They have to! Darkness can't stay in the same place with Light.

The Lord was with me, too, when I told my teacher the truth out in the hall. Mr. Lofton believed me!

And anyway, I think he knew who really did it.

And anyway, I think he knew I could draw much better pictures than *those!*

WHEN YOU DON'T KNOW WHAT'S AHEAD

Remember,
GOD IS WITH YOU

WHEN IT SEEMS LIKE NOBODY UNDERSTANDS YOU

Remember, God is with you

Did you ever have a very, very favorite book? If you did, then you probably knew those pages so well that when someone was reading it to you, you knew the next words before they were spoken. You knew what the next picture would be before someone could turn the page.

God knows us even better than that.

Did you ever have a favorite room and know where everything was in that room—even with your eyes closed? I remember my grandparents' old white house in the little valley like that.

I can close my eyes and hear the old oil stove click-click-clicking as it heated up in the morning. I can see the wooden lamp made by Great-uncle Isaac and the lampshade that was a picture of a lady at a lake. I can see the old white swivel chair that sat in front of the two big windows with a view of the fish pond and the old apple orchard. I can see the little brown desk with the clear, orangey plastic handles and the drawer where Granny kept her list of "odd names" in a brown spiral notebook. I can see the closet where they kept their toys: the red plastic shaver that really buzzed, the jigsaw puzzle of an old mill, and the *Henry the Helicopter* book. I can step out on the front porch and smell the damp forest across the road and hear a quail call through the fog.

I loved that place. So even though the house is just an old wreck now, with sad, empty windows and grass growing up through the front porch, I can see it the way it was.

God loves you and me and knows us that much and more.

He knows everything about you. He could close His eyes right now (but He doesn't need to) and see the way you hold your mouth when you're puzzled about something. He knows what you like to doodle with a pencil. He knows your new favorite color—and all your old favorite colors, too. He's looked into every one of your hiding places. He's visited all of the imaginary places you make up in your mind. He's walked in your dreams. He's felt the disappointments you've felt and never told anyone else.

Now, other people may not understand you at all. You may not even understand yourself sometimes. But there is Someone with you who understands you very, very well.

He *made* you, remember? And nobody loves you more.

WHEN YOU THINK ABOUT CHRISTMAS

Remember, God is with you

When it comes time for Christmas at your house, does your family do certain special things every year?

If you do, then those special things are called "family traditions." Once you've done something a few times over a few years, it's sometimes nice to keep on doing it that same way. (Unless you're stuck on some tiresome tradition that everybody keeps doing but nobody really *likes*. That's called a "rut.")

In our family, we listened to Christmas carols on the radio every Christmas Eve. I'm not sure what radio stations do now, but when I was little, they played lots of good Christmas music on that night.

We would turn off the lights in our living room...the tree lights would trace soft reds and blues and greens and golds into all the corners...the woodsy smell of the tree would weave itself through the fragrance of baked ham and candy canes and fresh bread and angel cookies and other good things in the kitchen.

And—just for a while, not very long—we would all sit together and listen to the music.

Maybe that doesn't sound too exciting to you—not like watching a video of Rudolph the Reindeer meets King Kong—but I liked that tradition very much. Sometimes the music would pick me up and carry me right *into* the Christmas carol. (I don't know how else to say it.)

> O little town of Bethlehem, how still we see thee lie!
> Above thy deep and dreamless sleep, the silent stars go by.
> Yet in thy dark streets shineth the everlasting Light;
> The hopes and fears of all the years are met in thee tonight.

Suddenly—for a minute or two—I wouldn't be in that little house on Marion Lane in Eugene, Oregon. Instead I would be back in time, and far, far away. I'd be flying over Bethlehem on a still, velvety night. I'd be out over the cool, inky dark fields, seeing the shepherds around their little fires and the huddled bunches of sheep. I'd feel the stillness of those places in my bones, like the stillness of starlight, and the wonder would well up in my throat.

Because

> ...I would know
> ...that something BIG was going to happen
> ...very, very soon
> ...maybe before my next breath!

What kind of big something? Oh, something better and brighter than anything that had ever happened before. I could feel it. I could sense it. It was just about to tear through the curtain of night. An explosion of clear, golden joy.

Something was coming.

Someone was coming.

Someone was about to enter the world, and nothing would ever be the same again.

> Fall on your knees! O hear the angel voices!
> O night divine! O night when Christ was born.
> O night! O night, O night divine!

The Son of God was about to enter the world He had made. And He was coming back as a tiny, helpless baby.

Why did He do it? Why did He come? The Bible says:

> He became flesh and blood...born in human form. Only as a human being could he die. And in dying he broke the power of the devil, who held the power of death. (Hebrews 2:14, SLB)

He came because it was the only way to save us from our sins. He came because He wanted to be with us.

WHEN YOU'RE FEELING SAD AND ALL ALONE

Remember, God is with you

Some people talk about angels coming to help them in troubled and lonely times.

That could happen! After all, the Bible says:

> All the angels are spirits who serve God
> and are sent to help those who will receive
> salvation. (Hebrews 1:14)
> (And that means you and me, if we belong
> to Jesus.)

But I remember a time when I was in trouble and God didn't send an angel to help me. Now, He could have if He'd wanted to. He has plenty of angels to spare, and they are very good, strong helpers. If an angel ever offered his help to me, I'd take it in a heartbeat.

But most of the time, I think the Lord would rather send one of His own sons or daughters to help us in our troubles, instead of an angel.

But this is the strange part: that person He chooses to send may not be the sort of person you imagine He would send. If you're not careful, you might not even recognize the very person He has sent to help you!

In a very frightening moment, God sent a person to be my helper.

He sent a lady.

A wonderful lady.

A lady with no hands.

I was with a group of people from America who love Jesus, and who were on their way to Romania to help and encourage people with some difficult physical problems. On the way, our plane stopped in Zurich, Switzerland. A group of Christians met us there—many with their own physical challenges. Some couldn't walk the way most of us walk. Some couldn't speak the way most of us speak. Some couldn't hear or see the way most of us hear or see.

But there they were to welcome us to their country in the name of Jesus. Switzerland never had better ambassadors. What a time we had that day! We sang and laughed and talked as if we were all old friends—even though we had never seen each other before. I learned something wonderful that day: When someone has the same God and Savior that you do, that person can never be a stranger. You don't even have to speak the same language!

The sweetest lady of all was a young woman who had been born with no hands. But once you saw that smile of hers—bright as the morning sun shining off new snow—you forgot all about the hands.

Right in the middle of this special visit, though, I heard some news that took the laughter right out of me. The airplane to Romania was full! Someone from our group would not be able to go on that plane. And that someone, I found out, was going to be *me*.

I had to stay behind while my group went on to Romania. I had to find somewhere to stay, wait for another day, and fly to someplace called Yugoslavia. After I got to Yugoslavia, I would have to try and catch a flight to Romania...if I could.

And I would have to do it all by myself.

Yugoslavia? By myself?

But what if I got stuck there? What if no one knew English? What if I didn't know where to go? What if they didn't like Americans? What if I couldn't catch up with my friends? What if I had the wrong kind of money? What if...? What if...?

I wish it weren't so, but I have one of those faces that always looks just the way I feel. Everyone was looking at me, and I think my face was looking pretty upset. My stomach felt like I'd just swallowed a baseball.

There was nothing my friends could do, so I tried to say good-bye to them with a brave face. I watched them get on the plane without me. I watched them close the door. I watched the plane taxi toward the runway.

It's hard to explain how alone I felt in that moment.

Alone in a strange, foreign place.

Alone, and not really sure where to go or what to do.

But I really wasn't by myself. The Swiss lady with no hands stepped up and smiled that smile at me again. "Oh Larry," she said (only when she said my name it sounded like music: "LAH-ree"). "Oh LAH-ree, do not worry. Do not be afraid. This will be wonderful. You can stay at my house. You can meet my friends. You can see a little of Switzerland. You can have hot chocolate. We will have such a good time. You will see." (I'll bet *real* Swiss hot chocolate is something special.)

And right away she walked with me to the airline counter, took my ticket in her two handless arms, and began speaking rapidly in her own language with the agent. What a help she was! (You don't need hands to help—just a willing heart.)

She arranged my flight and took care of all the details. She was just about to sweep me off to her Swiss chalet for some of that chocolate when we heard my name over the loudspeaker.

I was being paged. There was ONE seat open on the flight to Romania after all, and the plane was waiting on the runway. A whole planeful of people waiting on the runway for *me?* The Swiss lady grabbed my arm with her arm. "Run, LAH-ree! Oh, let's run!"

We ran like crazy (I had no idea where I was going). We ran arm in arm until we came to an exit. When I looked through the door I couldn't believe my eyes. There was a gleaming white jeep with a red-and-white Swiss flag on the door and a flashing blue light on top (the kind of car I imagine an angel might drive). And the jeep was there to drive *me* out onto the runway to the waiting airplane.

I looked back at my friend (the *real* Swiss Miss), and she waved at me...a sweet wave of the arm...a wave that had no hand and really didn't need a hand.

I will probably never see her again until I get to Heaven. And how will I know her? She will have two good hands then. But I'll bet when she says, "LAH-ree," and waves at me, I'll know who she is. And we'll have a cup of heavenly hot chocolate together (with whipped cream white as a cloud). And then maybe we'll drive around those golden highways together in a white jeep with a flashing blue light; I don't know for sure.

If we see you along that road, we'll give you a ride, too.

Our wonderful God is with us whenever we feel alone. He will always send someone to be with us...maybe an angel, or maybe a very special someone.

He's a Father who never leaves His children alone.

WHEN THIS WORLD COMES TO AN END

Remember, God is with you

e everything new

Have you ever thought about the end of the world? The Bible tells us that just as the world had a beginning, when God sent it spinning into deep space like a bright blue-and-green marble, so the world will also have an end.

The time will come when God says, "Enough," and the old creation will be over. One man in the Bible explained it like this:

> "Lord, in the beginning you made the earth. And
> your hands made the skies. They will be destroyed,
> but you will remain. They will all wear out like clothes.
> You will fold them like a coat. And, like clothes,
> you will change them. But you never change.
> And your life will never end." (Hebrews 1:10-12)

Just like your mom pulls the old sheets off your bed and puts on fresh, crisp, clean ones, God will roll up the old creation. And when He shakes it out in one good shake, *everything* will be new.

New galaxies.

New stars.

New planets.

A new earth with new forests and mountains and valleys.

And a new *you* in a new strong body to live on it!

Is that a scary thought to you, knowing that the old world (which everyone works so hard these days to save and conserve) has to END? Yes, it can be a scary thought. What will it be like?

When you come to the end of a book, you close it up.

When you come to the end of a telephone call, you hang up.

When you come to the end of a movie, you get up and leave.

What will it be like at the end of the world?

It's always a little frightening when we think of familiar things being changed. It shakes us up a little. I remember the first time I saw Mount St. Helens after the big volcanic eruption that tore off the top of the mountain.

I used to love to look at the mountain before the eruption. I worked at a business where I could see the mountain in the distance...the way it used to be. In the summertime, I would eat my sack lunch on a grassy hillside, under a lazy willow tree, looking off at that perfect, cone-shaped peak in the north.

Then I moved away for a couple of years. When I moved back and saw the mountain from our U-Haul truck, I was so startled I almost drove off the road. It looked as though some giant with a great ax had whacked off the whole top of the mountain. Big things like mountains aren't supposed to change like that!

And what will it be like when it's time for the WHOLE WORLD to change? What will it be like when God shakes out the old creation and makes everything fresh and new? I like what David said about such a time. He doesn't sound afraid to me!

> God is our protection and our strength. He always
> helps in times of trouble. So we will not be afraid if
> the earth shakes, or if the mountains fall into the sea.
> We will not fear even if the oceans roar and foam,
> or if the mountains shake at the raging sea.... Nations
> tremble, and kingdoms shake. God shouts, and the earth
> crumbles. The Lord of heaven's armies is with us. The
> God of Jacob is our protection. (Psalm 46:1-3, 6-7)

Wow! The Lord of Heaven's armies! The great General of ten million times ten million shining warrior angels. He is WITH us. He will bring us right out of the old world and into the new one.

If you know something more exciting than *that*, I'd like to know what it is!

WHEN THE PATH BEFORE YOU IS DARK AND DANGEROUS

Remember, God is with you

My nephew Robert loves to do things with kids. It's a good thing, too, because he's a youth pastor.

One time he went on a hike with six middle school kids from his church. Robert wanted to show them one of the coolest places he'd ever seen. It's called Blue Pool, and if you ever saw it, you might think it was the coolest place, too.

It's a place where the swift, powerful McKenzie River suddenly leaps up from under the ground and thunders down into a deep, ice blue, crystal clear pool.

You'd love this hike. In the fall, vine maples carpet the pathway in red and gold and squirrels hop from branch to branch chattering at you. The trail's only a few miles long—and worth every step of it.

So Robert and the kids were going to start early on a Saturday morning and drive up into the mountains where the trail starts.

But you know how that goes.

EARLY for some people means sunrise. EARLY for other people means "sometime before noon." So they didn't get away on this little trip when they wanted to get away. By the time they arrived at the trailhead, it was already afternoon.

But it was going to be a short hike—just a few miles—and wouldn't take much time.

But you know how that goes.

The kids goofed around, walked slow, took too much time eating their lunches, and, well, it took a long time to get to Blue Pool. Longer than anyone thought. By the time they got there, the sun was already sliding down behind the mountains.

But that's okay, because experienced hikers *always* come ready with flashlights and extra batteries, so they can find their way back in the dark.

But you know how that goes.

One of the boys had left his flashlight in the car. A girl had left hers at home. Someone else had a flashlight with no batteries. And someone else had batteries that wouldn't fit anything.

Darkness came fast. You could almost see it come—like someone turning a dimmer switch.

Have you ever been out in the deep forest away from city lights and car lights and streetlights and house lights and sign lights and every other kind of light? It isn't just dark, it's BLACK. You can wiggle your fingers right in front of your face and not see a thing.

So how were the kids going to find their way back? Were they frightened? Yes! There were some steep places and narrow places on that trail, where someone might fall. Was Robert frightened? Very much! The kids were his responsibility. (You have to be a grown-up to understand how scary *that* is.)

But Robert knew God was with them that night. Robert knew that even though *he* couldn't see, God isn't bothered at all about seeing in the dark. He remembered what David said in one of his psalms:

> Even the darkness is not dark to you [Lord].
> The night is as light as the day.
> Darkness and light are the same to you.
> (Psalm 139:12)

So the little group prayed together. "Lord, it's awfully dark and we're afraid of this darkness. But we know You are with us right now! Even in the woods. Even in the dark. Please help us find our way back to the car. Be our Light and our Guide. In Jesus' name, Amen."

Now, the Lord could have sent an angel with a big blazing torch, and I guess that would have been an exciting story.

But that isn't what He did.

Instead, He gave Robert the wisdom to know what to do. (And when you think about it, wisdom *is* like a light that helps you find

45

your way.) Robert had each person grab the waist of the person in front—just like you'd do with your friends if you were pretending to be a train. They began walking carefully down the trail through the brush and trees.

Sometimes the "train" went straight ahead, with Robert as the engine, and other times the train turned a little sideways as they all felt carefully for the trail with their feet.

Trusting in the Lord, no one panicked. They sang all the praise songs they knew, and the group became a Praise Train, chugging along through the darkness.

Finally they made it back to the car, and no one was hurt or even scratched. (But now I'm very sure Robert carries a flashlight and extra batteries *wherever* he goes!)

Flashlights weren't even invented when David was a shepherd boy in Israel, but he had something even better. He wrote:

> Even if I walk through a very dark valley,
> I will not be afraid because you are with me.
> (Psalm 23:4)

Sometimes, whether we like it or not, our path in life will be dark. Sometimes it will seem like we are just feeling our way along, because we can't see what's ahead.

But David had the right idea. (And so did Robert!)

Praise to Jesus can light up any dark pathway. And there's no room for fear on the trail when He walks beside us.

WHEN YOU SAY GOOD-BYE TO SOMEONE YOU LOVE

Remember, God is with you

The Best Reunion Ever

died and had given it to his wife as a present. She kept it outside her classroom in the courtyard, where she could see it every day. When Mrs. May found out what had happened to her planter, she cried.

I'm not sure why, but Steve and I didn't get into much trouble for that. (I think we *should* have been in trouble, don't you?) But I've often thought about that time in the locked courtyard. I was already a Christian when that happened, and—deep down—I knew God was always with me. But when I got scared, I forgot to remember those things. And because of my fear, I made a foolish decision that hurt someone very much.

That's the way it is with bad decisions. People you never meant to hurt get hurt. Things get broken that can't always be fixed.

I need to turn to God *first* in those scary times, not afterwards, when I've made a big mess of things.

The God who was a Friend to Isaac in his new neighborhood is my Friend, too. Next time I forget that...I hope you will remind me.

55

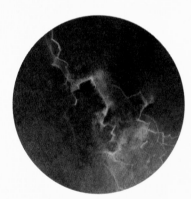

WHEN YOUR BEST FRIEND MOVES AWAY

Remember, God is with you

Of all the treasures you might find or uncover in a lifetime of living on our world, finding a friend who loves Jesus is just about the best. Two friends who both love Jesus can be closer than any other two people can be. Do you know why that is? It's because He is holding both of their hands at the same time. And even though they might let go of each other from time to time, Jesus will never let go of either of them!

Some friendships last a few weeks. Some last a year or two. Some last many years or even a lifetime. But a friendship in God is much longer than that. A friendship in God reaches right out of this world and into the world to come.

Of course it does! And then it just keeps getting better and better through all the adventures and fun of our new forever home. Did you know you will have new friends and old friends in Heaven?

Of course you will! You might make new friends with any of the millions of God's children who lived on earth from the beginning of time. You might be friends with a boy who grew up in the days of Abraham or Moses. You might explore a fun little planet with a girl who lived in long-ago China before anyone ever thought of a country like ours. You might even make friends with angels who've lived in Heaven all their lives and never visited the earth even once. (And of course they'll want to know everything you can remember about it.)

It's wonderful to find new friends, and I don't think we'll ever run out of them in Heaven. But that doesn't mean there won't be time for your best and closest Christian friends from your own years on earth.

Any fun and laughter and closeness you shared together on this earth will be so very much better in that better place.

Just imagine a fresh, shining morning in Heaven. (I think it must always be morning there, don't you?) You find yourself walking along a path of soft, sandy gold through rolling fields of wildflowers under a sky so pure and blue you feel like you could drink it. (And maybe you could!) For some reason, you find yourself thinking about your good friend and suddenly—in the twinkling of an eye—there he is, or there she is! Right in front of you and ready to be with you and hike the trails of Paradise with you.

I know a little girl who had a club with her best friend from up-the-street-and-around-the-corner. Missy and Emily called their club The Christian Kindness Club, or T.C.K.C.

Now, I was never very sure what this club was for and what it did. But *they* knew! They made signs with crayons and colored pencils that said T.C.K.C. and decorated them with sunshine and flowers and rainbows and happy faces and other special, secret things. They would hang these signs up wherever and whenever they had their meetings.

And I was never very sure just what went on in their club meetings. But I knew that one of their favorite places to meet was on a slender white branch up in our family's birch tree. You would see one of their colorful club signs hanging on a bush and you would look up and—sure enough—there they'd be. Up there in the tree with birch leaves rustling around them and the flowers and ferns down below them, dangling their bare feet and chattering like a couple of birds on a telephone wire.

Sometimes when it was raining they would put on fancy dresses, start up a Christian praise tape on the stereo, and dance around our living room, standing on their tiptoes and whirling their dresses around.

They didn't like anybody else to watch them very much (especially older brothers who didn't understand), but I could tell by the way their eyes sparkled what a wonderful time they were having. Sometimes their dancing was very serious. But most of the time they were giggling their heads off!

Then one gray, rainy day in September, Emily had to get into a big orange-and-gray truck with her family and move all the way across the country. There were hugs and tears on that day, and not all of them belonged to the little girls.

Now these girls don't see each other anymore. They write letters now and then and draw pictures for each other and send each other dried flowers or sticks of gum, but there are no more meetings of T.C.K.C. up in the birch tree on fine sunny days. (I think that birch tree misses them. The leaves whispering in the summer wind sound a little lonely to me now.)

There are no little girls swishing and swirling long dresses together and giggling and dancing to songs about Jesus in the living room.

But I have a question for you.

Does that mean their love for each other is "gone"? Does that mean The Christian Kindness Club is "gone" forever? If it has gone, where did it go?

If you ask me, I don't think it's gone at all. It really doesn't matter if these two little girls become young ladies with other interests and other friends. It doesn't matter if they become grown-up women with busy jobs or husbands and families of their own in faraway parts of the world.

Someday those two girls who shared such a strong love for Jesus and for each other will be together in Heaven. And in that place, whether you are a child or a grown-up won't matter so very much, because grown-ups will be as happy and carefree and full of fun and joy as little children.

And if there are nice birch trees on earth with good branches for sitting, there are much better branches on much finer and higher trees in the light-dappled forests of Heaven. The flowers are prettier and the wind sings sweeter songs and summer days never get dark or turn cold.

And if you think there is beautiful music that honors Jesus here, wait until you hear the music there! *No one* will be able to keep from dancing! Not just in a living room by a stereo but out into

rivers of light and over mountains of clouds and through rolling fields of rainbows and out among the shining stars.

Oh, there will be such meetings of The Christian Kindness Club in Heaven. Such fun! Such dancing! Such happy talking and singing—with no one to spoil the fun or tease. When angels see the hand-lettered signs that say T.C.K.C. they will fold their wings and walk by quietly so as not to interrupt.

I think the Son of God Himself will be a member of that club and no matter how busy He may be, He will never miss a meeting.

Friends in Jesus are friends forever.

When your best friend wants to be with you, what does he do...what does she do? I knew what my best friend Steve would do. He would come flying up our front steps two at time and knock on our door. "That's Steve," I would say, before I ever opened the door. And I would be right.

It might be after school, or it might be after breakfast on a gray, rainy Saturday. And I was so glad to open the door and see him and invite him in. We had such fun times together...playing Monopoly tournaments...throwing the football around...riding our bikes to Skinner's Butte...doing fake radio programs on his tape recorder. We laughed, wrote songs together, drew pictures, listened to Herman's Hermits and Beach Boys records, skipped rocks on the Willamette River, did imaginary superhero stuff, and maybe (once or twice) even talked about girls that we liked (he liked Delaine and I had a major crush on Barbara Brown).

Now what if one rainy day I heard Steve's familiar knock on my door and decided not to open it? What if I just let him stand out there on the front porch in the rain, knocking and knocking?

Well...I wouldn't be much of a friend, would I? That's no way to treat someone who takes the trouble to come to my house and knock on my door just to be with me! How could I do that to such a good friend?

Did you know that Jesus Christ, the mighty Son of God, has been knocking on the door of your heart? Did you know that He has been waiting and waiting for you to invite Him into your life and be your Savior?

Here is what He says in the Bible:

> "Look! I have been standing at the door. And I am always knocking. If anyone hears my voice and opens the door, I will come in. I will fellowship with him and he with me." (Revelation 3:20, SLB)

Now, maybe you've already invited Him in. I hope that you have. I will never forget the day when I opened the door and invited Him into my life. I was only nine years old, but it was the best and most important thing I have ever done. What wonderful times we have together. He is my *real* Best Friend.

But if you have never invited Him in, guess what? He is still outside your life, He is still knocking, and He still wants in.

Do you know why?

BECAUSE HE WANTS TO BE WITH YOU.

Just think of that! The God who created you and everything there is wants to be with you.

He wants to be your Savior and Lord.

He wants to be your closest Friend.

He wants to be with you forever in Heaven.

But there is something between you and God that keeps you apart. That something is called sin. Our sin makes us an ENEMY of God, and the Bible tells us that *all* of us have sinned.

> All people have sinned and are not good enough for God's glory....When someone sins, he earns what sin pays—death. But God gives us a free gift—life forever in Christ Jesus our Lord. (Romans 3:23; 6:23)

If God hadn't stepped in to rescue us, our sin would have separated us from Him *forever*. No one could get to Heaven.

But do you know what God did? He sent Jesus to live with us and then to suffer and die for us. Jesus paid the price for our sins that we could *never* have paid. Jesus said:

> "For God loved the world so much that he gave his only Son. God gave his Son so that whoever believes in him may not be lost, but have eternal life." (John 3:16)

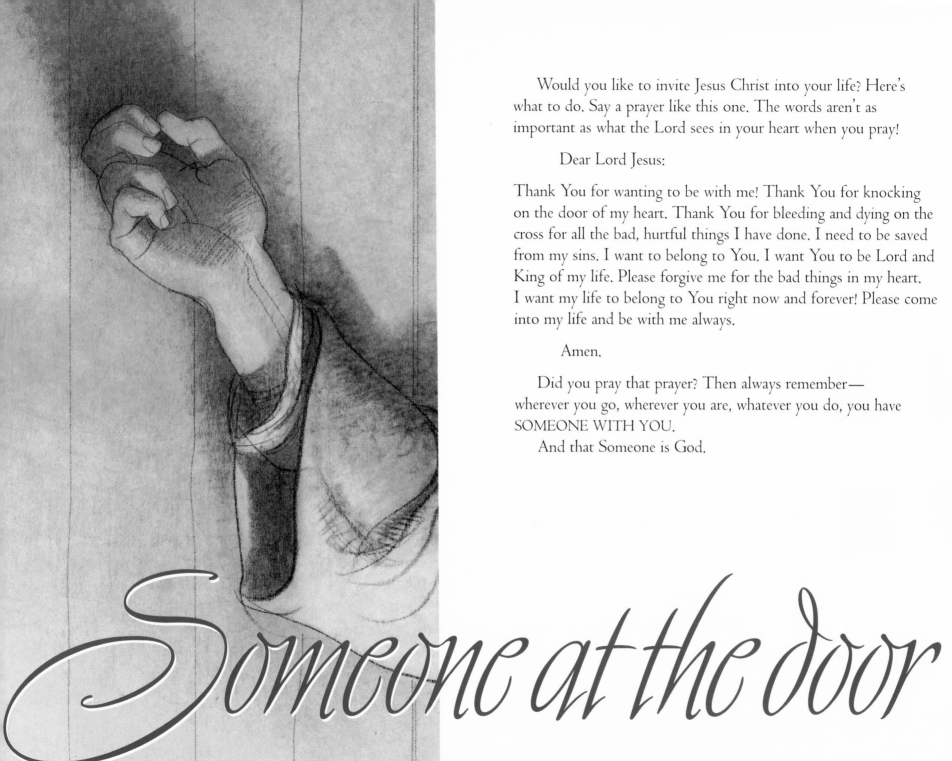

Would you like to invite Jesus Christ into your life? Here's what to do. Say a prayer like this one. The words aren't as important as what the Lord sees in your heart when you pray!

Dear Lord Jesus:

Thank You for wanting to be with me! Thank You for knocking on the door of my heart. Thank You for bleeding and dying on the cross for all the bad, hurtful things I have done. I need to be saved from my sins. I want to belong to You. I want You to be Lord and King of my life. Please forgive me for the bad things in my heart. I want my life to belong to You right now and forever! Please come into my life and be with me always.

Amen.

Did you pray that prayer? Then always remember—wherever you go, wherever you are, whatever you do, you have SOMEONE WITH YOU.

And that Someone is God.

Someone at the door

SOMEONE WITH YOU
published by Gold 'n' Honey Books
a division of Multnomah Publishers, Inc.

© 1998 by Multnomah Publishers, Inc.
Illustrations © 1998 by Sergio Martinez

International Standard Book Number 1-57673-317-3

Printed in Mexico

The author gratefully acknowledges Kevin Keller,
a man with "eyes of the heart," and the designer of this book.

Most Scripture quotations are from:
International Children's Bible, New Century Version
© 1986, 1988 by Word Publishing. Used by permission.

Scriptures marked SLB are from *The Simplified Living Bible* © 1990.
Used by permission of Tyndale House Publishers, Inc.
All rights reserved.

Gold 'n' Honey is a trademark of Multnomah Publishers, Inc., and is
registered in the U.S. Patent and Trademark Office.

For information:
Multnomah Publishers, Inc.
Post Office Box 1720
Sisters, Oregon 97759

Library of Congress Cataloging-in-Publication Data
Libby, Larry.
Someone with you / by Larry Libby.
p. cm.
Summary: Uses anecdotes and situations from daily life to illustrate
that God is present at all times, especially when one is sad, lonely,
fearful, hurt, or facing a particular difficulty.
ISBN 1-57673-317-3 (alk. paper)
1. Presence of God—Juvenile literature. [1. God.] I. Title.
BT180.P6L53 1998
231.7—dc21   97–51805
                              CIP
                              AC

99 00 01 02 03 04 05 — 10 9 8 7 6 5 4 3 2